Searching for Home

~ↄ

Elizabeth Mateer

A Publication of The Poetry Box®

Poems © 2024 Elizabeth Mateer
All rights reserved

Editing & Book Design by Shawn Aveningo Sanders
Cover Design by Shawn Aveningo Sanders
(cover photograph courtesy of Chris Lui via UnSplash)

No part of this book may be republished without permission
from the author, except in the case of brief quotations
embodied in critical essays, epigraphs, reviews and articles,
or publisher/author's marketing collateral.

ISBN: 978-1-956285-72-7
Published in the United States of America
Wholesale Distribution by Ingram Group

Published by The Poetry Box,® October 2024
Portland, Oregon, United States
website: ThePoetryBox.com

for Katie

Contents

7 | Daughter Blue
8 | Seasons of One's First Apartment
10 | Ramen Shop
12 | Serendipity, Postponed
13 | Fractured
14 | 9th Street
17 | Sonnet for a Bad Cat
18 | to stop moving in fear
19 | Dark Side of the Moon Child
21 | Two Faces
22 | James
24 | Under the Joshua Tree
26 | Vernio
28 | Snow in New York / Sun in California
30 | Attachment Wounds
32 | Bella Marie
33 | Chapter 2
34 | Chapter 1

37 | Early Praise for *Searching for Home*
39 | About the Author

Daughter Blue

I yearn to be loved like the songs,
I remember believing when I sang.
I used to sing
America the Beautiful, with pride and
love for country.
Daddy, why did you abandon us for loyalty
to mother? As she'd prefer to be referred.
Return the belief I could be loved
as you never did.

Seasons of One's First Apartment

My body slumps,
half-lying on the bed, the hot tile floor creating a pool
of sweat under my bare feet.
No A/C.
Just July summer heat.
Focused
on the brown spot staining the ceiling.
It's grown, I think.
Hot tears stream down seventeen-year-old cheeks
in Jersey.

Spring had come before, when I realized
the unregulated heat.
And the promise of beginning had started to wane
with $20 to my name
in Jersey.

I'd been so proud of this place,
with the cream-tiled floors,
and the dirty stall shower.
"first house on the left,"
in Jersey.

    Winter was sweet
    in cozy two rooms.
    A tabletop Christmas tree.
    Wrapping presents, writing cards.
    Homemade Rice Krispy treats.
    Sparse, with low ceilings,
    but home.

I'd walked around the house
for the first time in October.
Before I realized the sparking pebbled steps
were just crumbled.
Seventeen years old,
in a basement apartment
in Palisades Park,
New Jersey.

Ramen Shop

Inconspicuous, minus the neon OPEN radiating out onto 6th street.
We make our way through the miso fog.
Finally, arriving, you suck in your breath and climb
into our table, dingy at the back,
avoiding obstacles of others pushed too close—
when was the last time they washed this?
We're stuffed in this corner, sitting with another couple of strangers,
keeping our elbow tucked—this is definitely not up to code
sitting here looking at you.

Remember the first time you tried ramen?
You thought I meant the 33-cent dried packages
bought at the bodega for a dollar in New York.
Dining to doo-wop and the continual *plop* of drips in the steel sink
   behind us.
               …life could be a dream
                               sh-boom sh-boom…

Struggling with red plastic chopsticks to keep hold
of the thick noodles' slippery sides.
Mine are spicy, yours are not.
You lean close, parting the flavored mist—*how lucky are we?*
      —to have met in another world, and be here.

And now you're back, back in my city,
in this shop that seats less than thirty.
Where we perch on rickety wooden chairs and whisper,
where soup slurps splash and we're thankful we didn't wear white
   shirts.

And now it's our place,
and every day it's full,
this noodle shop and my soul,
in the heart of Alphabet City.

Serendipity, Postponed

soft as a naptime awakening, fingertips brush over skin in exploration
hesitant, as if you fear I might bruise or disappear from your bed
my head rests in the crook of your arm, slowly reaching to feel
the chest hairs that curl over the neckline of your gray t-shirt
my chin lifting towards the stubble on your cheek, warm
safe in the scent of whiskey, sweat, straw, and cotton
touching that spot on my ear I told no one; precise
your hand glides, submerging under my shirt
versant as a bird that knows the water; your
clothes cling, taunting my imagination
breathe deep; I keep from moaning
skin and nerves and bones vibrate
endorphins; movement hesitates
safe is unexpected. I freeze
laughter in the other room
we laugh too, moved
from the moment
breathe deep
not
yet

Fractured

All I want is to be pretty and make art.

The very box I spent myself fighting
to climb out of
became a home

that I can no longer go back to.
And again,
I am lost.

The pain of not caring for the mundane
but caring too much about being perceived.
Extorting shame is power.
Avoiding shame, maybe more.

The facade of existence is so overwhelming
truth only free in shadows
under poison

avoiding the wrong of ourselves
denial is intoxicating.
So split the deck
and hide
the undesirable cards
until you're so   fractured
you no longer recognize yourself.

All this time
Chasing legitimacy, approval, tax returns,
love from my mother.

But I'm with the rats and no amount of table manners will change that.
I play it well though, you wouldn't know.
And repeat the lie—I like it this way.

9th Street

I noticed the scaffolding that had been covering the entire corner
of a building for the past three years was removed.
I'd never seen the naked building before.
But there it was, standing on its own,
polished stone shining in the streetlight.

I'd moved into an apartment on 9th Street and Avenue C
a year after coming to New York City.
It was more my home than anywhere else I'd lived, at the time,
in my mind, both because I'd lived there the longest and because
I paused and allowed myself to settle. In the tiniest room I'd ever lived.
My yoga teacher said that we are mentally attached
to every item we own through our subconscious.
A little bit of energy for everything; the less we have, the freer we are.
I believed that.
So I piled all of the stuff I needed in a van and
left the rest in Queens,
shedding.

I loved my street.
9th is lined with cafes that are not Starbucks,
small clothing stores that don't carry name brands,
vintage shops, and bars.
The guy at The Bean knew that I wanted hazelnut coffee,
it's closed now.
People said 'hi' as I walked down the street,
making my section of the city feel like home.

Very slowly, my home began to shape.
I chose furniture that fit
the dimensions of my space.
I bought my first grown-up bed.

Changed the hardware on my dresser from silver to gold.
Found a pink rock salt lamp and Japanese incense.
My sanctuary in Manhattan.

As frustrated as I became with New York,
when returning to my neighborhood, and then my home, I felt
    grounded.
On down days, a walk-through Tompkins Square Park,
an everything bagel with olive cream cheese,
watching the pups in the dog park turned right.
They were just as happy to chase a ball in the sunshine or the rain.
Kids skateboarded on the basketball court,
the man who rode the mountain bicycle with the giant tires blasting
hip-hop music from an old stereo strapped to the back created the
    soundtrack.
It smelt like wet dog and damp sawdust.
On weekends, bands played music in the center.
I tried to stop and listen. It's always been a strain to go slow.

I walked around the north side of the park
on the south side of the street to admire the painted brick
townhouses and avoid the excess rats at night.
I still squeal like a child when one runs out of the darkness
too close to my foot. Those moments,
when leaving and returning home, tracing my steps
on the hexagonal sidewalk bricks, if there isn't a rush, were my favorite.

Slowly, I continued to live in the buzzing hub, and shed.
It started with just things, excess material objects.
But then became people,
jobs that weren't good for me,
commitments that sucked my soul.
Because New York sucked at me so much
there wasn't enough left to be had by anything
that made me less than happy.

Crammed wall to wall with eight million
strangers and I was becoming a minimalist.
Was it freedom, or just continuous bailing to prolong
my drowning?

Sonnet for a Bad Cat

He sits, arms crossed and folded
Finally content in the day, it would seem
After havoc and ruining more than esteem
Calm in amnesia of when he was scolded
Content as he knows his master is molded
To care, despite every scene
While forced to continue to clean
Fresh urine-soaked laundry, just folded.

Yet, behind each act that is out
There is fear beyond the show
Of being misunderstood and alone
And so, despite their daily bouts
Not if, or why, they know
That each is the other's home.

TO STOP MOVING IN FEAR

more than beauty or resilience or art
coming up against smart reaches a fear
so deep
it touches where my attachment ends

because you will know

    but where intelligence leaves so does respect

    and you can fuck what you don't respect
    for a time
    but you can't love
    and then it's over
    and what did we learn

so I wonder
if this could be different
because you are
    and I am trying to be

I don't want my wound to win
maybe I will let you perceive me
    maybe I can grow

Dark Side of the Moon Child

I am Artemis.
But this shell I live in doesn't fit.
We all have our box.
And so Aphrodite was archetyped
upon my frame. Sexuality to entice
gods and men alike.

And yet, I thought I was seen for a time.
We played like children in the desert,
wind whipping dirt-caked faces
our laughter echoed in the canyons.
Tears streamed from squinting in the one o'clock sun
a juniper berry burst between my thumb and index
herbal and lingering, rub my nose, joy in the wild.
I didn't think of gin.
I'm real.

But at night
we searched for the stars and could not find them.
You were clouded,
preying on the vulnerability
I allowed you to see
because I thought I was safe.
And again,
I am perceived as nothing but my shell.
Existing for sex
I was told,
in no words.
A beautiful idiot.
You can fuck what you don't respect, right?

Child of the moon
trapped in Venus.

But you see,
this tender heart knows rage.
How could it not?—
when all the world has shown is power and violence.
And you forget, under this disguise of beauty and desire
she speaks beast and has perfect aim.
These are the moments that shape us
into shadow or light.

The dark side of the moon child
playing in the wild with
who she thought was a friend
forgetting she is prey—
is the rage of a huntress
with no mercy.

But shoot your shot. My quiver is ready.

And all you will ever see is Aphrodite.

Two Faces

You speak with me,	Your ability to remain silent is astounding.
in all of your words.	No words, even less.
Yearning to know the wild, paint-spattered incohesive parts	Indifferent to the existence of
that somehow coalesce	who you've touched, just
and you are enamored,	absorbed in self-pity and avoidance.
Safe,	I'm afraid
with you	of who I'd be had you stayed.
I see your wounds, too. Masks over shells, vigilant of what moves around us. They wouldn't know. But I do.	
I see you. You said to me, in all of your words.	
	I wasn't enough.
Sometimes I don't disinfect a cut because I want to feel the pain and risk sepsis and death. Self-harm by omission, I've always loved a loophole. But I don't anymore.	I still do.
And for the first time in my life, I'm afraid to die	And again, death holds the only promise of relief
because I don't want to be without you	because you are gone.

James

We climbed. Looking back, I noticed,
your grin—way too wide—
to disguise your fear
    of falling.

We should have known.
Thin air and gravel underfoot,
a path above the clouds,
elevation requiring the trees to grow horizontally
before reaching for the sky.

Unprepared for what we'd attempted.
Improper foresight and moving too quickly
up a path to nowhere.

Half of a second in a moment I knew
what you didn't want me to,
you were afraid.
But you let me. And it was OK.
And we found another route, and pressed on
despite shame, miscalculation,
and poor footwear.
Facing what was ahead.

As we climbed, slower this time,
between a few too many jokes to assuage
the discomfort of what is new
what was vulnerable
and unknown
to the sound of cowbells,
beyond mountain pastures the color of astroturf
that we not, in fact, astroturf,

It occurred to me that I could one day love you.
We made it to the top. Signed the book.
Checked it off.
And finally, after far too many miles,
      descending,
            driving,
                    as the wind caressed our faces
in that obscure countryside
with the top down and radio up
you sang that James Taylor song
and a yearning for family,
intangible beyond craft,
appeared out of whipped air.
And I knew,
I would.

Under the Joshua Tree

The chilled summer desert air
is blowing dust into our painted cups
of red wine.
While a wool blanket, wiry
hugs our shoulders and
the pungent scent of gas igniting hits our nostrils.
Canned fire flickering in front
of our plastic chairs
pushed into a makeshift bed.
Under the Joshua Tree.

Polaris in our eyesight, it's 2am.
Jetlagged roosters telling us when
we giggle to struggle to breathe.
Outside a stickered trailer decorated
with skeletons and dollhouse food.
Your laughter enveloping me into your mouth.
It's gentle now.
But don't poke your eye
on the spindle of the Joshua Tree
searching for the north star
because I'm right here, basking in the light
of your existence, knowing
that we are honey overflowing
and sticking to your chest hairs.

The magic of now is overwhelming,
simultaneous existence in millions of years
and we are the lucky ones.
I never imagined you thought the way you do,
I only am starting to know,
I think I see the beginning of how much.

And yet you wane—in silence and highs.
Afraid? Of what—
we are both searching, and here.

I never thought I love you so much.
I love you so much, under the Joshua tree.

Vernio

Dust-covered and beaten,
our cream Fiat approached the top of a steep gravel road
at a yellow villa, the one you chose.
It felt like coming home.

We tiptoed into the pool at midnight.
My legs found your torso and wrapped, as did my fingers
through the short strands of your hair. Your arms carried me in circles
and our mouths melted under the Tuscan stars of my ancestors.
Sparkling, as I learned the world did with you.

The only two in existence,
minus the old man watching Italian game shows on the patio.
You said you were cold, that surprised me.
Though now it doesn't so much.

A bottle of chianti fiasco and you asked a question.
Softer and timid, in a tone I hadn't heard, outside your usual brusk.
I felt it—hopeful?
A wall down, if only for a moment. I could hurt you.

Entangled under a patchwork quilt that night, cool mountain air
    drifted
into the old bones of the house, twisting around our young bodies
and the iron wroughts of the bed. It felt like home.
Not a movement through the night, frozen and melting simultaneously
into what I would eventually call,
My favorite memory.

Midnight sparkles reflect what occurs when you let in.

About memories, context and hindsight inevitably shifts.
To be warped or clearer?
My desperate aversion of looking back
in loss, worried that
I'll never remember without the taint
of who you turned to be.
Or else, lose my favorite memory.

So I choose when. To remember that short-lived vulnerability
when you felt like home and I realized it wasn't a place.
Even so, I will go back to those mountains alone.

I wonder if the stars will still sparkle?

Snow in New York / Sun in California

I didn't know her name.
Just that she was thirty-two years old and driving to California
to check into a hotel and kill herself.
That's where she was from.
She didn't want her family to go to a great expense
to move her body afterward.

The snow was falling in chunks outside
the sixth-floor window,
gathering in piles on the rooftop across the street.
I pushed against the desk with my foot
and leaned into the old blue swivel chair,
back support long gone and untangled the phone cord.
Those cords were always tangled.

She was resolved.
Don't worry, I'm not going to do anything on the phone,
she said. I don't want to traumatize anyone.
She felt guilty that dying would cause her mother pain.
I asked what her biggest concern was.
Even though she's been cruel to me, she's still a person,
she said. I don't want to cause another human pain.

The snow was falling slower, in bigger chunks.
My chest felt the realization, she was sincere.
Most callers have hesitations, doubts, are in immediate crisis.
She was calm.
Her plan was well-thought out and deliberate.
She was going to do it.

The snow fell swiftly to the east, pressed by the wind.
It was cold, but not as cold as you might think.

Everyone had a snow day, Manhattan was closed.
I stared at a faded plaster wall painted the color of hardboiled egg yolk.

I wish I'd found your service earlier,
she said. Maybe it would have helped, you are all really nice.
It's hitting me that this is my last week on earth.
There's no one else to talk to, you know,
you're probably one of the last people I will talk to.

The snow was accumulating on a wiry, leafless tree.
The light faded outside the window as the seconds hand
on my brown leather watch kept the same pace
while the minute hand progressed faster than usual.

She wanted to set up a tent on the beach and die watching the stars.
I asked her why she wasn't planning her death that way.
I don't want anyone to find me and try to be a hero,
she said. That will only make things worse.
The only control I have left on this earth is when to leave it.
She was crying.
I've taken up a lot of your time,
she said. I should probably go.

I didn't want her to go.
I told her to please, please call back at any time,
we take calls 24 hours a day.
She said she might.
The call ended at 33 minutes.
As soon as I hung up,
the phone rang again.

Attachment Wounds

A world out to get us—no.
Just playing out relationally
the way it always has.

Fighting
our very nature, how we were raised.
Or not.
To trust, to cling, to fear
         abandonment, freedom,
your hand

in order to stay alive, to grow.

I fear losing my freedom.
The ones loved, always fearing
         abandon—
all of them
I did.

Protecting the child with so much love to give;
Those big feelings were dangerous.

we learned
break off those pieces
hide them well
         in the shadows
fractured existence
               unknowable
but safe

and the child grew
to be a villain

rejection of the self is power
at a cost
maybe that's why
the antagonist is always searching for a mother

Bella Marie

Vanilla caramel ice cream swirly girl
in personality and presentation.
Formally, a pastel tortoiseshell.
To friends, my beauty queen
trash cat. Grizabella Marie.
With tiny white socks
and marble toe-beans. Somewhat short
in stature for your frame. Wanting yellow eyes,
your face too round, due to the appearance given
by fluff, as if you have cheeks.
Always earnest,
eager for love and grateful
when it is given. You know cold,
the streets of Brooklyn weren't kind.
But now you curl daily
at 101 degrees
on a pillow just for you, next to me.

Chapter 2

You don't understand, you make me less lonely.

Holding my hand across the table
as I struggled to not cry for the third time over tea.
We developed slowly,
no rush—our souls know.
Between paying and playing, this love is sacred,
impenetrable by men
or money.

Two lost, abandoned by family
Searching for home in New York City.
Why does it so often take leaving to know
where you belong?

I admire how you always think there's more time.
You make me more present.
You don't show your sadness though—
only tell me after.

You're afraid to grow old but I look forward
to being old after a life lived with you,
not lonely.

Chapter 1

A chance meeting underground after French
You claim cheating, but je ne parle toujours pas français.
Style advice off the
68th Street—Hunter College stop.
Taking our lives in New York for granted.
2020 closed that. But not so obviously.

Now, you're closing doors on Newtown Avenue
and the entire west coast can kiss my ass.
This is more defined. Formal, almost,
as if the plot has moved forward after some character development.

I am OK,
because of you.

Chapter 3 is still the beginning of the book.

Early Praise

Searching for Home is a portal that transports readers into Elizabeth's world, enabling them to feel the emotions she experienced in the moments she describes. Her words not only evoke her own feelings, but also resonate with other's experiences. Through her writing, I am able to share in and *feel* her moments of beauty and in her moments of despair. She masterfully captures a broad spectrum of human experiences and emotions. *"Two Faces"* and *"Attachment Wounds"* particularly resonate deeply with me. Take the journey with Elizabeth city to city, country to country, across her visceral experiences that we can all relate to. You'll laugh, your breath will catch, and you'll be taken back to a cherished memory of your own.

—Lynn Greathouse, author of *Swerve*

As I read through the book *Searching for Home* by Elizabeth Mateer, I often wonder, "When was I in New York, eating ramen, walking the streets, feeling the city's pulse? When did I live out these memoirs?" This collection paints vivid pictures of personal experiences, emotional landscapes, and everyday settings, offering intimate glimpses into the author's life and mind.

The opening poems set the tone, resonating deeply with me as they evoke feelings as if seeping through like a warm cup of coffee, filling me with new experiences. Particularly poignant is "Seasons of One's First Apartment," where the physical discomfort of a sweltering, budget strained life parallels the emotional and financial struggles of early independence. "Ramen Shop" transforms a simple meal into a symbol of connection and nostalgia. A cramped setting contrasts with the warmth of shared moments, turning ordinary experiences into cherished memories. Meanwhile, "Serendipity, Postponed" explores intimacy with a mix of tenderness and restraint, capturing a vulnerable moment in time.

Each poem, distinct in voice and perspective, draws readers into contemplative spaces where personal histories and emotional truths unfold with lyrical grace. The poet's ability to extract beauty from pain and find significance in the mundane showcases the transformative power of poetry.

—**Christopher Olivas McPherson, poet**

About the Author

Elizabeth Mateer is a poet whose writing sinks into human relationships and the resilience of the human spirit. Originally from New York, Elizabeth's thirst for adventure has led her to all seven continents, enriching her poetry with a global perspective. Her work is heavily influenced by her personal experiences with grief, imbuing her poems with a raw, emotional depth that resonates with readers. Elizabeth holds a Bachelor of Arts in creative writing from Hunter College. Currently working towards a PhD in clinical psychology, Elizabeth continues to explore the complexities of the mind, both through her professional work and her poetic expressions. Her poetry has been featured in the recent anthology *Fractured Light* and *Beyond Words Literary Magazine*. In addition to writing poetry, Elizabeth is also a translator and ambassador of Italian poetry for The Poetry Lighthouse. At home, she finds joy and companionship in the presence of her two beloved cats.

Instagram: @SearchingForHomePoet

Website: SearchingForHomePoet.com

www.ingramcontent.com/pod-product-compliance
Lightning Source LLC
LaVergne TN
LVHW050028080526
838202LV00069B/6960